SUBURBAN
RENEWAL

SUBURBAN
RENEWAL

Tom Connor

Viking Studio

Acknowledgments

The author is indebted to the following people for their support and help. Lisa and Jack Connor, George and Del Grenadier, J. Barry O'Rourke, and Laura Campbell. Also to the photographers Robert Benson, J. Barry O'Rourke, Robert Perrin, Joseph Kugielsky, David Todd, and Dan Cornish.

Thanks are due Emily Gordon, Dave and Libby Hibbs, Sue Cutler, Philip and Yael Eliasoph, Ellen Hyde Phillips, Judy Procter, Pam Lloyd, Susan Albright, Wendy Benson, Ann Kugielsky, Diane Jones, Richard Fitzgerald, Alice Sinkevitch, and Mary Cooperman.

I am particularly grateful to the architects and contractors who generously contributed their time, projects and plans, especially Joe Matto, Ed Clemente, Jonathan Wagner, Duo Dickinson, Steven and Cathi House, Dale Mulfinger, Patrick Pinnell, Sarah Susanka, Tony and Joanne Amenta, Doug Garofalo, Tony Terry, Craig Saunders, Jim Estes, Paul Harris, Mark Finlay, Jay Valade, Bob Harper, Rob Sanders, Ben Baker, Mark Hutker, Michael Farewell, Harrison Gill, Tony Ialeggio, Skip Broom, and Jim Ezzes.

Special thanks to Joel Fishman and Kevin Lang of The Bedford Book Works, Inc., and to Cyril I. Nelson at Viking Studio.

VIKING STUDIO
Published by the Penguin Group
Penguin Putnam Inc., 375 Hudson Street,
New York, New York 10014, U.S.A.

Penguin Books Ltd, 27 Wrights Lane,
London W8 5TZ, England

Penguin Books Australia Ltd, Ringwood,
Victoria, Australia

Penguin Books Canada Ltd, 10 Alcorn Avenue,
Toronto, Ontario, Canada M4V 3B2

Penguin Books (N.Z.) Ltd, 182-90 Wairau Road,
Auckland 10, New Zealand

Penguin Books Ltd, Registered Offices:
Harmondsworth, Middlesex, England

First published in the United States by Viking Studio,
a member of Penguin Putnam Inc.

First Printing, October 2000

10 9 8 7 6 5 4 3 2 1

Copyright © Tom Connor 2000
All rights reserved.

Library of Congress Catalog Card Number: 00-130356

Book designed by Laura Campbell
Printed and bound by Dai Nippon Printing Co., Hong Kong, Ltd.

Photographs of "California Modern," pages 92 to 97, courtesy of *House Beautiful*, copyright July 1992, The Hearst Corporation. All rights reserved. Christopher Irion, photographer.

ISBN: 0-670-89217-3

This book is for V. George McLaughlin

Architect, Engineer, Inventor, Grandfather

Contents

Introduction

This book might best be viewed as a weekend drive through the suburbs, looking at houses. The places illustrated here—late-1940s and '50s Cape Cods, '50s and '60s Ranches, '60s, '70s and '80s Colonials—were the building blocks of 20th-century American family life. Set down next to nearly identical houses in subdivisions across the country after World War II, they were designed to be as plain and predictable as Monopoly buildings. As you will see, they are near-perfect forms for altering, updating, embellishing, expanding, and individualizing, while keeping their owners in down-to-earth neighborhoods.

"People long for community and love the older neighborhoods," explains Sarah Susanka, a Minneapolis architect and the author of *The Not So Big House* (1998). "But they want houses bigger than what they have, and they want them to reflect their personalities. They're adding older architectural styles to the kind of standard houses that didn't have much style to begin with."

This trend coincides with a growing sophistication among many American homeowners and the current boom in home improvement. At the same time, the average price of homes in the suburbs has skyrocketed, eliminating trading up for a sizeable segment of the population. As with homeowners after the war, about the only houses available to many are older Capes, Ranches, and Builders' Colonials.

In the hands of less-imaginative owners and less-skillful architects, they would have been knock downs. But while young investment bankers and captains of e-commerce have razed older homes to erect monumental edifice complexes, many more homeowners have turned these once-modest development houses into one-of-a-kind homes of quiet charm, distinction, and value.

"Value is always about location," says Emily Gordon, a real estate agent with Riverside-Shavell/Coldwell Banker in Fairfield County, Connecticut, where a boom in transforming post-WW II houses is underway. "But in general it's wise in these houses to add a master bedroom, or expand the kitchen, or re-do the bathrooms. In this market, you'll always get your money back. And as the value of one house on the street rises, so do the values of the others. A house can be worth more just by being next door to a transformed Cape or Colonial or Ranch."

Many of the houses featured in these pages are in Connecticut, where I happen to live. But just as many can be found in other New England states, and in parts of the Midwest and West. Most of the renovations and expansions cost as much as the houses did when their current owners bought them (rarely did homeowners or architects share numbers, but approximate costs seemed useful). All this has at least given me and my wife some ideas for transforming our own house.

In the late 1600s, settlers began building small, compact houses up and down Cape Cod and in other parts of Massachusetts and Connecticut. These early examples were reminiscent of English and Dutch cottages, but they possessed a style of their own: a story-and-a-half high, with a center entrance and hall, an eight- to twelve-pitch roof and, as the style evolved, symmetrical dormers in front and frequently a shed dormer in back.

By the mid-1930s, the center-hall Cape had become the most popular house style in the country. G.I.'s returning home from World War II found them affordable and nearly ubiquitous. They were America's "starter" house.

But the very elements that made them attractive fifty years ago have become drawbacks for contemporary families. Rooms are typically small, low-ceilinged, and dark. Tight lots and steep roof pitches often limit expansion to dormers. Modest by their nature, the houses are plain and look pretty much the same.

Now, however, homeowners are finding Capes still relatively affordable and also ideal for transforming. They are adding formal entrances, prominent gables, larger windows, and exterior molding, and opening up the interiors with big rooms off the back. In the process, they are turning common "starter" houses into singular "finisher" homes.

▪ C A P E S ▪

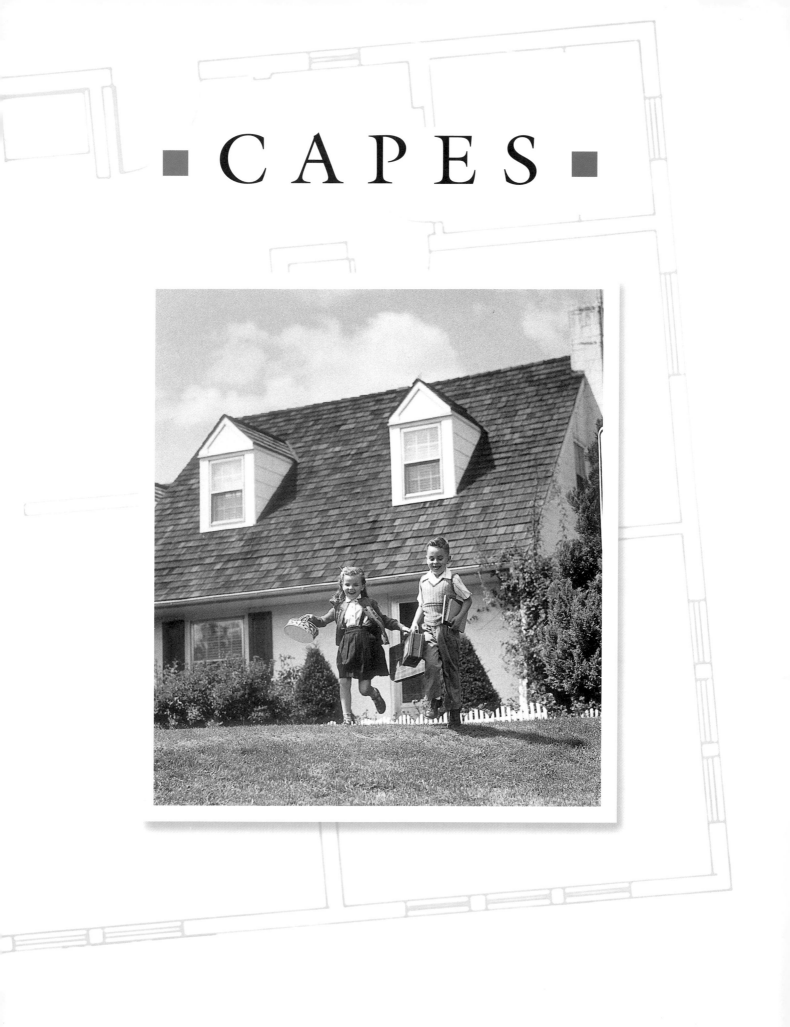

Detailed Cape

When Ed Clemente and his wife, Leigh, bought a run-down Cape dating from the late-1940s a few years ago, he knew exactly what to do. For one thing, he grew up in a neighborhood of post-World War II houses four blocks away. For another, he's an architect.

Ed hired a contractor to knock down a back porch and push out the rear wall of the tiny kitchen, then added an expanded kitchen/family room with a cathedral ceiling. Upstairs, he ran a shed dormer off the back—a time-honored way of gaining space in Capes. And since these houses are typically cramped and dark, especially on the second floors, he set an open cupola into the roof above the staircase, giving the illusion of raising the low ceiling and letting in light.

Out front, borrowing elements from Shingle style "cottages" in Newport, Rhode Island, the owner-architect enlarged and exaggerated the existing gables and replaced the small dormer windows with over-sized squares to break up the long, horizontal line of the facade. The center cupola and circular window in the main gable appear to anchor the house to the site and serve as nautical references to the beach community to which it belongs. To date, the renovation and expansion—an ongoing project—has cost about half the price of the house. It has also influenced two other Cape transformations that appear in these pages.

It's all in the details: Staggered gables, Tuscan columns, boxed rakes and rake returns transform this once-plain '40s Cape, inset.

Photography: J. Barry O'Rourke

Craftsman Cottage

Richard Abramson, a coppersmith, had worked on half a dozen houses designed by Edmund Clemente, whose own Cape is featured in the preceding pages. So shortly after he and Hillary Ward bought their 1947 Cape, Richard hired the architect to realize his ideas. "Everything I sketched just looked like I'd taken a Cape and stuck a room on it," he recalls. "I didn't want any one part to not go with the rest of the house—I wanted something subtle, I wanted something pleasing to the eye."

While the architect and owners refined the style of the house, Richard took three months off to work with a crew framing a new master bedroom and extended kitchen. They also replaced the roof to strengthen the rafters and steepen the pitch. Richard shingled the exterior and built the rear decking himself, but subed-out the electrical, plumbing, and heating, then bartered copperwork for the kitchen cabinets. And for five months during the most intensive phase of the interior renovation, he and Hillary lived in a rented trailer parked in the driveway.

Gradually, what began as a Shingle style house evolved into a Craftsman cottage derived from the American Arts and Crafts period. Ed flared the base of the house, created a dramatic gable in front and designed the highly stylized, ornamented dormers that accentuate the new Cape's romanticism and charm. Richard, naturally, added copper touches wherever he could: gutters and leaders, flashing, capped rake returns, window-box bands. He also designed the shingle weave in the apex of the large dormer— a pattern similar to those he'd seen on other old houses—and added other decorative touches.

Fine workmanship, an eye for period detail, and a love of natural materials separate this house from its past, inset, as well as from the other late '40s Capes on the street.

Under the eaves: The owner came up with the details —arches, a cross-weave shingle design, counter-sunk circles to break up the gable expanses—that endow the house with character.

Where Abramson and Clemente differed was at the front entrance. The architect likes classical columns, the owner doesn't. That got them into a discussion of brackets, which is more an Arts and Crafts-style detail than columns, and that in turn led to a decision to pitch the soffits of the front overhang and dormers in a manner consistent with the same architectural style. Richard found Craftsman details and lighting online; the period reproduction hardware and custom-made front door came from catalogs.

The clean simplicity of the house, and the integrity of the design and details, have given it a striking presence. "Richard really paid attention to details," Ed notes. "Some people cut back on them but he went in the opposite direction—he took them to a whole new level."

The extended kitchen and master bedroom, with the accompanying deck and small, gabled porch, bring the back of the half-century old Cape to life.

Photography: J. Barry O'Rourke

Gambrel Cape

The 1950s house was a 1,200-square-foot, odd L-shaped Cape—possibly (the architect isn't exactly sure)—that had been painted lime green. "When we moved in, in 1989, a lot of houses looked like this," explains the wife. "People said, `Why don't you knock it down?' But there was something funky about the old plaster walls that I loved."

On a young couple's budget, she and her husband added one room off the back with a builder, then hired Robert Sanders to expand and remodel the whole house in two more phases. "As long as you stay within our budget," she recalls telling the architect, "you can do whatever you want." Rob promptly added a second floor of three bedrooms and two baths, and chose a gambrel roof for its shape and efficiency, and also because it wouldn't overwhelm the scale of the first floor. At the same time, he gave the shadowy front door presence by extending the second-floor gable beyond it, then creating underneath an entrance corridor with thick columns. The effect is repeated on either side of the garage, where the columns appear to support another gable.

The third phase of the project involved what the owners call "Rapunzel's Tower"—a two-story staircase that leads to an office and a library over the garage and to the master bedroom. The three phases of renovation, spread over nine years, cost a little more than the original cost of the house.

Photography: Joseph Kugielsky

A gambrel roof and gabled overhand create an efficient second story and well-defined front entrance, below. In the back of the house, right, a central, projecting staircase leads to a library over the garage and a new master bedroom. The kitchen wing is far right.

Island Cape

Martha's Vineyard, the wedge of sand and scrub oak off the Massachusetts coast, is the fashionable summer home to presidents, entertainers, captains of industry and e-commerce, and socialites. But it has also long harbored a large colony of artists and writers, and in the wooded, off-the-beaten-path center of the island, two writers who had rented for several seasons recently scripted the perfect year-round retreat.

Or retreat*s*. Hearing about a funky place for sale up the road, the couple found three one-room cabins and a Cape-style, single-story cottage next door. All were rundown, but the largest of the old cabins sat perched above a pond—something the island's strict building codes wouldn't permit today—and the cottage had already been approved for a major expansion and renovation. The writers bought all four buildings.

Now all they had to do was turn the rundown places into a charming compound of related structures. The couple hired Mark Hutker Associates, a Vineyard architectural firm, and local contractor Andrew Flake. The existing Cape, which was completely renovated, became a two-bedroom, two-bath guest house. Adjoining it, linked by a window-lined corridor, is a two-story addition that houses the new kitchen and living room on the first floor, and a master bedroom and writing room on the second; the renovated cabins are also used as writing and inspira-

Hybrid House: Traces of Cape, Colonial, Shingle style and Victorian architecture meld to form an eclectic Island style.

Exterior photography: Bob Schellhammer

tion rooms. Authentic-looking materials—antique pine floorboards, native stone, used doors and doorknobs, beaded-board ceilings and walls—give the new-old Cape a seamless, well-lived-in feeling.

"The goal was to create an instant heirloom," notes Mark Hutker. "The porch was designed to look as if it had been built on, filled in, then opened up again. It's a fictional reading of the evolution of a house."

The style of the house today is indigenous to Martha's Vineyard: Shingle style with elements of Capes, Colonials, Victorians, and old camps. "It's sort of a '90s retreat or camp," says Philip Regan, the project architect on the job, "but it's also clearly eclectic—most of the architecture out here is. We were trying to take it back in time, and trying to play down the scale of the building instead of having it be something that pushes itself on the island."

Looking as if it has always been here, a new porch off the addition fully appreciates its location.

The new living room, below, appears older and more authentic than the original, inset. The native-stone fireplace, built by island master mason Lew French, recreates the atmosphere of old camps on Martha's Vineyard.

Timely Addition

Even for a young couple without children, the 1,600-square-foot developer's model felt cramped. Like hundreds of similar houses built throughout the New York metropolitan area from the 1930s to the '50s, it borrowed its mass and scale from Cape Cods, and its roof pitches and façades from English Tudors. Rather than move from a neighborhood they liked, the couple decided to add on and called in Connecticut architect Mark Finlay.

The architect designed a 750-square-foot addition that includes a new kitchen and breakfast, dining, and family rooms. He used steps and columns between the rooms to define the separate areas and their functions. French doors at the end of the addition open onto a backyard that was previously ignored. Above the addition is the master bedroom. "It's a simple space," the wife says, "but we wanted it to be done right and we couldn't quite visualize how it would look. Mark kept the lines of the house—there's nothing abrupt about the addition—but he put a lot more details into it."

That was a dozen years ago. The day they signed the contract for the addition, which cost roughly a third of the house's purchase price, the wife learned she was pregnant with twins, now eleven. And the architect has since become nationally known for designing big, expensive, traditional homes.

In a narrow house on a narrow, shaded lot, a young couple blew out the rear wall, and expanded and renovated the interior. The project turned three small rooms into one big space, letting in light and making room for a family.

Photography: David Todd

On the exact site of the old Cape, inset, the new house spreads out
across the cliff and opens itself completely to the sea.

Coastal Rambler

Not long after settling the New England coast, people began building Cape Cods—low, small-windowed structures that could take a nor'easter in the face without blinking. Even as late as the late-1940s and early-'50s, when the house that this used to be went up on the rocky coast of Rhode Island, it seemed appropriate that it be a Cape.

Since then, of course, a few things have changed. The original house, which had just two bedrooms and a 550-square-foot living room/dining room/kitchen, had grown in value by the early '90s to around $100,000. But the spectacular site was now worth five times that. Coastal restrictions would have prohibited a new home from being built so close to the cliffs and water, so when the house changed hands in 1993 and the new owners wanted to renovate, they were naturally after a home that would be equal to the site.

The trick for Newport, Rhode Island, architect James Estes was to double the size of the original house and maximize the views while preserving the cottage-like feeling of the Cape, and satisfying zoning requirements that any renovation should have a low profile.

Jim's design ingeniously achieves all this. He preserved the relationship of the house to the site by creating a series of single-story, scaled buildings similar to the original Cape. Where a few small windows once allowed a peek at the Atlantic Ocean, banks of glass doors and side-by-side double-hung windows now open the entire interior to the view. Where the land slopes away to the

Beyond banks of French doors, awnings, and both double-hung and hinged windows, stone terraces and wood decks extend the living space in the front and back of the new house to the edges of the rugged, waterfront property.

left, Jim was able to build a two-story tower above the attached garage that holds the scale but serves as a focal point of the house and site. Surrounding wood decks and stone terraces follow the contours of the cliff. In the end, despite doubling in size and changing in character, the house still looks as if it belongs on the coast of New England.

As if designed for a different planet , the new interior is all about room and light and full views of the water.

About Face

Years ago, when this Cape predated the street it presently fronts, the main entrance looked down acres of lawn and meadow to the main road. However, once the land was subdivided and a new road built, the front of the house became the side, the side became the front, and the back became the other side. More confusingly, since the new driveway passed the former back door, visitors now began taking this for the front door and walking directly into the tiny kitchen. The owners spent four years guiding friends to the living room before dialing architect Anthony Amenta's number for help.

Aside from needing a real front entrance, the couple wanted a large family room—something most Capes never had. And since both husband and wife are Southerners, they wanted front and back porches. At the same time, it was important to them that any addition look akin to the original Connecticut house.

Tony's solution was a 1000-square-foot wing that's built perpendicular to the small Cape and completely reorients the combined house to the site. He accomplished this by uniting the old and new behind a veranda (to use the Southern vernacular) along what is now the front of the house. Like so many other new porches gracing post-W W II houses, this one relies on a gable to mark both the new, recessed front entrance and the marriage of

The original porch, inset, on the side of the old house; the front door was to the right. The new porch ties the existing house to a large addition and emphasizes the reoriented main entrance.

the two structures. A vaulted dormer window above the entrance also defines the center and softens the sharpness of the house's multiple gables. The front door opens into a wide hallway between the original house and the wing; it runs from front to back, leading to a second, shorter porch.

The wing itself is a single room with a cathedral ceiling, triple sets of French doors on opposite walls, and aligned sets of three dormers on each roof slope. "We played around with a bunch of different ways to bring light into that tall room," says the architect, "before realizing that the simplest thing to do was these dormers, which gives the room scale and a repetitive element the roof needed."

The wing and porches cost about $75,000 in 1991, the year they were added.

Photography: Robert Benson

The 1,000-square-foot wing is naturally lit and ventilated by matching trios of French doors at floor level and dormered windows above. Quarter-rounds set into the end gable let more light in. The dormers also help keep the new house, which nearly doubled in size, looking like a Cape Cod.

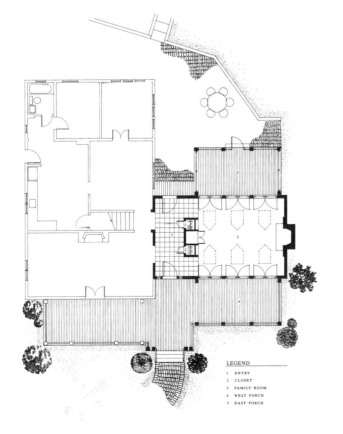

The first-floor plan shows how new front and back porches enclose the addition, further opening up the airy room. As a result, the former front entrance, inset, turned and receded to become a back door.

LEGEND

1 ENTRY
2 CLOSET
3 FAMILY ROOM
4 WEST PORCH
5 EAST PORCH

Classical Cape

Phillip and Yael Eliasoph aren't traditional Cape dwellers. He teaches college art history, she Italian. They're more Mediterranean than New England, more classicists than suburbanites. But they wanted to be close to the beach; a late-1940s Cape six hundred feet from Long Island Sound was the closest place they could afford; and they had seen what architect Ed Clemente had done with his own Cape nearby (see Detailed Cape, page 10). They bought the old house in ten minutes.

Quickly, Phillip sketched his vision of the new front entrance, and he and Yael agreed on the ideal interior: as open as practical, with as many windows as possible, but with wall space for a sizeable art collection. Then they turned to a trio of professionals to make it happen. Ellen Hyde Phillips, a design consultant, worked with the couple on the interior design, moving walls and taking down a closet to make room for a large painting. Ellen, in turn, worked with architect Harrison Gill and Connecticut builder David Raymond.

In effect, the team turned a five-room first floor into a single, airy, lemon-lighted space divided only by the central staircase and attached closet. "It's the defining feature of the house," says Harrison. "It took a lot of structural gymnastics. We basically had to tear out the whole backbone of the house and conceal the new support structures. But when you walk in the front door, you can see straight through the house to the gardens, which is amazing in a Cape."

Exterior photograph by J. Barry O'Rourke

At the same time, Ellen's interior design separates the space into small, cozy areas. Deviating from the blueprints, David opened up the top of the stairwell, raising the second-floor ceiling two feet and adding a skylight, to ease the transition from downstairs to upstairs. He and Phillip also widened the vestibule, portico, and front steps, making them more welcoming, and added double windows on the western side of the vestibule and extra-wide sidelights on either side of the front door.

Thus, what was once a New Englander's winter lair has blossomed into an open-air villa on Capri. "I call it "Palladio by the Sea," says Phillip. Adds Yael, "This was a dark hole. Now the house is all about light."

Guests were originally greeted by the center-hall staircase. Now they are welcomed into a vestibule that brims with space and light.

Five small, dark, downstairs rooms became one. Below,
the living room flows from the vestibule through French
doors to a deck off the back of the house, inset, before.
The light-flooded family room was once a garage.

Nautical Influences

"It was an odd house," architect Donald Richardson says of the late '50s' spec Cape near the Rhode Island coast, "a combo of post-and-beam and Modernist, with the ugliest interiors I've ever seen. The materials were at the low end of the scale and it was really dark." Fortunately for his clients, they already knew that. They felt the same way, in fact, and even before the closing on the house had hired Don to renovate, expand, and modernize the place.

Here, a coastal-pond-and-shore way of life, shared by other families in a small compound of similar houses, set the design parameters. The owners didn't want to go above the existing roof's ridgeline. But both husband and wife—he grew up on Cape Cod, she in Rhode Island—wanted to reorient the dark house to the salt air and to views of the pond and the ocean, four hundred feet to the south.

Their architect pushed through the roof, adding gables, flat sections and shed dormers, to gain seven hundred square feet of living space. Just as important, in the process he broke up the monotony of the solid saddle roof, and gave the profile of the house a nautical—and Cape-ier—feel, befitting the site. He also used oversized clapboards, inspired by Danish barques, and ship-like pipe railing on the front and rear decks.

A ship-like deck, pipe railings, and elevated walls of windows
respond, in the renovated house, to the ocean 400 feet away.

"I'm not really sure what style the house is now," Don concludes, "but it has Scandinavian and nautical influences, and I think really captures the essence of the owners, who are nautical people and modernists. Its verticality, and the way it cuts into the landscape, is like a boat. It's a rough metaphor for a life close to the coast, and a trim, clean, simple but elegant solution to the problems found in the original house."

The renovation and addition, although small, cost the couple about two-thirds the amount they paid for the house in 1997.

As late as the 1950s, coastal New England homeowners sheltered themselves against the elements, inset.
In the late '90s, the new owners opened their doors and windows to them.

Photography: Robert Perron

New Wave Cape

All the couple with three children wanted of this elongated, 1,700-square-foot Cape was a fourth bedroom, a home office of some kind, and a little more space in the kitchen and master bedroom. Oh, and one more thing: When talking with architects about what the expanded house might look like, the wife mentioned "something daring—not a traditional, boring Colonial." In Chicago architect Douglas Garofalo's vocabulary, that translated instantly to signature Garofalo touches: off-beat materials, bold geometric shapes and strong colors.

"Without any nostalgic attachment to the style of this building, there was a desire to take advantage of these banal conditions," notes the architect, "so that each room, existing or new, became 'characterized' as a loosely connected collection of parts, no two of which are alike. The house then becomes extroverted in an episodic way." Or, as Chicago A.I.A. Executive Director Alice Sinkevitch puts it, "he blows Capes up and puts them back together again."

Despite mutating beyond recognition, the new house retains much of the scale and linearity of the original Cape, inset.

Photography: William Kildow

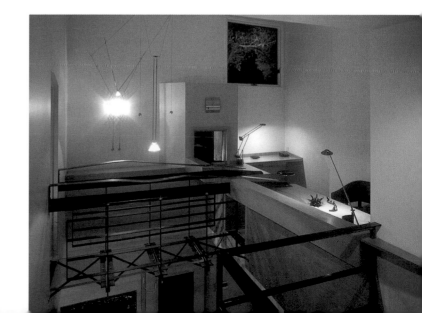

A two-story family room, far left, angles for maximum height and light off what was once a flat, nearly windowless rear wall, inset.

Basically, what the architect did was to replace the buttoned-down, symmetrical, white house with big, colored, play-blocks of synthetic stucco and squares of open glass. The new windows bring light into the center of the house, not just the periphery, and help define the open interior. Doug also enlarged the children's bedrooms over a new, attached garage and workshop; designed a two-story-high family room and single-story sunroom off the back; expanded the master bedroom into part of the new family room space; and engineered the steel and acrylic bridge that leads to a small office created by opening up a former closet and raising the roof above it.

Despite nearly doubling in size, the contemporary house has more or less the same scale and relationship to its neighbors as the old Cape had—much like a punk or New Wave child of conservative Republican parents who, nonetheless, remains a member of the family and one of the kids on the block. The project, completed in 1994, cost under $100 a square foot.

High above the front entrance and main stairwell, a steel and acrylic bridge connects the master bedroom to a small but high-ceilinged office.

Ranches—or "ramblers," as they are called in the Midwest—grew out of several distinct house styles: Japanese architecture, the California bungalow, and the Prairie Style as exemplified by the work of Frank Lloyd Wright. Perhaps the structures represented modernism for young homeowners in the 1950s, or symbolized the American dream. Whatever the reason for their appeal, with single-level floor plans, low-pitched roofs, and unadorned façades they quickly spread out across the suburban horizon as if there were no end to the landscape, and no tomorrow.

Eventually, the style lost its freshness and became, like so many of the "before" houses shown in these pages, nondescript. But the basic nature of the Ranch lends itself to renovation, expansion, and some of the most imaginative and dramatic transformations in this book. "Clients don't say, 'I want to turn my house into a Ranch,'" observes Dale Mulfinger, an architect in Minnesota. "They may say, 'I want to take my Ranch house and turn it into a Cape Cod.' But most people say, 'Is there any chance you could make it look more charming?' There may now be a style out there called 'charming.'"

As you can see in the following pages, what were once nondescript '50s and '60s houses are now Victorian, Colonial, Craftsman, and Contemporary homes of great freshness and charm.

·RANCHES·

Classically Modern

This one-story structure, probably built in the 1920s, has been many things to many people: a teahouse, a small ski chalet (sited on top of a hill fifty miles north of New York City, it has views of lower Manhattan), and home to numerous families. Over the years the house grew wings and gables, including the '40s-fancy front entrance shown in the "before" photo above. But it took an Australian musician and record producer from California to thoroughly transform the house—it's now a contemporary, two-story, 6,000-square-foot mansion—and, in the process, show how an imaginative entrance can set the stage for big changes inside.

Architect McKee Patterson designed an entrance big enough to contain a formal front hall with powder room and coatroom, and grand enough to signal a sense of arrival to the new house and twenty by forty-foot living room. He replaced the gabled entry with a high, U-shaped vestibule and convex front wall, then added an arbor with wired-glass canopy.

The hall is a mix of the traditional and the modern, the serious and the not-so-serious. Curved moldings and fluted pilasters are formal touches, as are the flared and fluted columns at the edge of the vestibule, which hide air ducts. But the zinc balls resting in molded pockets at the top of the columns, and repeated elsewhere on the first floor, break up the formality of the room. "It was just fun," the architect explains. "It got rid of the seriousness of the whole thing and put a little whimsy into the room."

When this 1920s Ranch, inset, turned into a stone mansion recently, the main entrance was transformed, too. Lit by clerestory windows, the new vestibule, right, sets the stage for the big entertainment room beyond.

Exterior photography: Adrianne de Polo

European Cottage

Like many other properties in these pages, this ordinary 1947 Ranch occupied an extraordinary piece of land—2.3 acres of woods and lawn overlooking a marsh and pond. When a couple of empty-nesters bought it in 1995, they did so understanding the house's potential. What they envisioned were the country cottages they'd seen in their travels through England and the south of France, and that's what they asked architect Joseph Matto to recreate for them in the south of Connecticut. "This is a collage of all those cottages they loved," Joe says.

For better or worse, much of the existing house was badly rotted and had to be torn down. An existing wing, built in the '70s and jutting out on the left side of the house, was also removed (the owners moved into a nearby condo during renovation).

This 1947 Ranch, inset, went back in time; the new design was influenced by old stone cottages the owners fell in love with on their travels abroad.

Starting practically from scratch, Joe raised high the roofbeams, doubling and steepening the gables in front and hipping the rest of the roof on both sides (the inverted flairs at the ends are reminiscent of old roofs in France) to balance the house and pull the eyes to the center. There, an exquisite, twelve-foot-wide eyebrow dormer focuses the overall cottage effect and also serves as the primary window in the new master bedroom.

The materials used also reflect the couple's well-traveled tastes and sensibilities. The roof is wood shingle and the majority of the façade is made of quarried stone and fieldstone taken from an old wall on the property and mixed in a style known as Celtic Bond. The front entrance, projecting two and a half feet from the larger gable, features a wood canopy with copper roofing. The custom door, rounded in the cottage style, is mahogany.

Inside, the architect took antique beams salvaged from a church in Canada and created a mortise-and-tenon cathedral ceiling for the new, enlarged country kitchen. Although the original footprint (i.e., a building's perimeter) was reduced by five hundred square feet, the size of the house was increased by seven hundred square feet. More important, it now has a fitting relationship with the site and views.

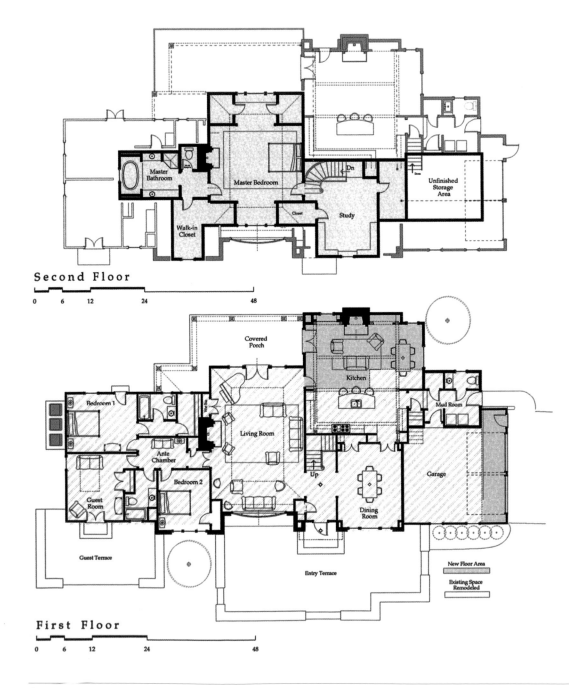

Second Floor

0   6   12   24   48

First Floor

0   6   12   24   48

Empty-nesters, the owners have the new second floor entirely to themselves; the broad, eyebrow dormer brings light and water views directly into their master bedroom. Only the kitchen is new space (the solid pink areas of the floor plan); the rest of the first floor was completely reoriented and remodeled.

In the renovated country kitchen, where owners and visitors spend the most time, mortise-and-tenon beams salvaged from a church add drama and meaning to the cathedral ceiling.

California Craftsman

Peter Blake had a California dream: He wanted to live in Marin County in a house with a view of San Francisco. When a small place with that potential came on the market in 1994, he asked a friend, architect Steven House, to look the place over with him. "Essentially it was a one-story '50s Ranch," Steven recalls, "with small windows, dark, dated rooms, shag carpet, and aluminum-frame windows. But if you stood on the flat roof, you had this incredible view of the mountains and the bay and San Francisco. Peter walked to one end and said, 'I want to put my bed here.' Then he took a chair and placed it in another section and said, 'And this is where I want the toilet.'"

Actually, Ranches being Ranches, the second-floor addition—a master suite with cathedral ceiling and a roofed-terrace—proved the simplest part of the renovation. The suite straddles the entry, creating soaring, two-story spaces connected by a bridge; it is lit by walls of Arts and Crafts-style windows, clerestories in the ceil-

A Brady Bunch-style Ranch, above, reinterpreted in the Craftsman tradition—with views, for the first time, of San Francisco Bay.

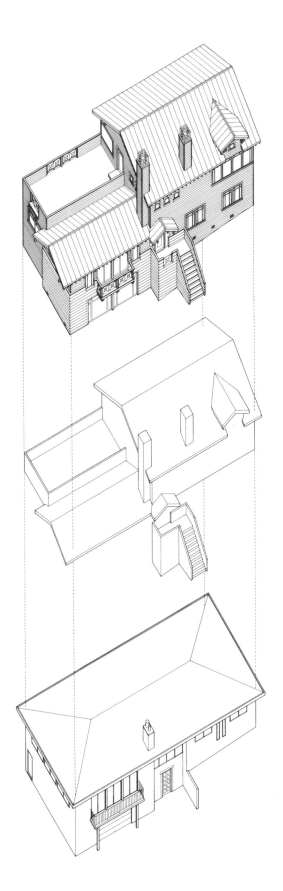

The house evolves, above. Raising the roof allowed the existing living room, inset, far right, to change, too—from an eight-foot ceiling to one sixteen feet high, with an open floor plan and augmented daylight.

The shag carpeting, above right, went along with the banister, railings and cramped kitchen, below. The new kitchen area, above, and entry hall, far right, re-invent the concepts of "greeting" and "entertaining."

ing, and a fireplace in a study area off the room. Steven also raised the eight-foot-high living-room ceiling, leaving the new wood trusses exposed, and blew out the original, basement-level front entrance to create a twenty-foot-high entry in its place.

The tougher challenge was to turn a cheap track house into a home that equaled the view. Because his client liked the Craftsman style, Steven reinterpreted it in a '90s' California manner. Nothing of the original Ranch, in fact, was left untouched in the renovation process. The architect stripped, gutted, refaced, and transformed the 1,800-square-foot Ranch into a 2,500-square-foot contemporary in the Craftsman style. True to that tradition, materials and workmanship are the real stars in this renovation. The base of the house is sheathed in ship-lap siding, the upper level with V-groove. Decorative wood brackets and thick eaves enrich the overhangs. The roof is copper, the railings wrought iron, and the windows steel-framed.

Photography. Gerald Ratto

Eastern Ranch

The Ranch style perfectly suited the domestic desires of this Connecticut homeowner, a classical violinist of Japanese descent. After her husband, a cellist, died and she decided to stay in the house, she sought what other owners in this book wanted—a home that opened itself to the landscape and welcomed the sunlight, but also one that would express her heritage as well as her profession. The limited budget she had for renovation fit the minimalist look she was after.

Japanese architecture and classical music informed the renovation of a '70s suburban Ranch, inset.

East meets West: Post and beam construction, native to both Japan and New England, coinhabit the redesigned interior. Rice paper panels in the doors and ceiling panels, above, however, clearly suggest the owner's heritage.

Architects James Childress and Paul Shainberg left the original roof in order to keep costs down, but added a low-gabled entry porch and flower wall to expand and focus the entrance, and a gabled wall of glass at the back of the house. The view from the entry now is straight through the house down a river of light that didn't exist before. Wood beams and columns connect the interior to the trees outside.

On her frequent trips to Japan, the owner collected Japanese shelter magazines that inspired the architects to marry East and West in the Ranch. Using local building materials and techniques, the design blends the character of Japanese farm buildings with southern New England country houses; in particular, the post and beam work represents both styles. In the interior American-made doors feature wood and rice paper panels, as do the panels in the living-room ceiling. The shaped kitchen cabinets echo the curves of a violin; elsewhere, woodwork is joined with bronze pins to resemble the instrument's tuning pegs.

Shingle Style

When it comes to their own homes, architects frequently think exactly like homeowners.

A dozen years ago, Anthony Amenta, a principal in Amenta/Emma Architects, P.C., and his wife Joanne, who works in marketing at the firm, went house hunting and in the process found a perfect structure to renovate. It was a late '60s, one-story Ranch set high on a third of an acre, surrounded by larger, older, two-story homes. All the couple had to do was add another floor.

"Putting a second story on a house is not cheap," Tony now says. "We would've been better off taking the house down to the foundation. We tried to save the first floor framing, and that's where we spent a good deal of time and money." The couple also wanted an older look to the renovated house, which meant details and materials—Royal cedar shingles, over-sized columns, circular windows—that were more expensive than they had thought. And as an architect, Tony had a problem with the existing front door which, in an L-shaped house, can easily get lost. "I wanted the door there," he recalls, "but I also wanted to create a sense of importance with the entry."

Adding nearly 1,700-square-feet above the existing house, he "stepped" a series of tall, gabled fronts back from the garage to

"Things in threes": Trios of stepped-out gables, dormers, and window patterns give the new house a sense of drama and completeness it lacked before, inset.

break up the mass of the new space. Directly above the garage is a new living room, and above that a two-story master bedroom. The third gable embraces a high entrance archway. "Things in threes look more dynamic than pairs," he notes. "The arch creates a front porch, and frames and accentuates the entry."

In the interior, Tony and Joanne kept the kitchen in the original location but expanded it into a former eat-in area. They also turned the old living room into a formal dining room. A steel beam traverses the first-floor ceiling, supported by a fat column. "It is chubby, isn't it?," Tony muses. "I don't know why. It just worked out that way—the column winds up in the middle of the floor in order to support the beam. A more delicate column wouldn't have looked as good."

The couple spent on the transformation about what the house itself cost to buy. And the architect learned a valuable construction lesson. "Frankly, adding a full story is difficult," Tony says. "If I had to do it again, I'd look for a house with a high enough roof or opportunities for taking advantage of unused space. It's easier to go out than up."

Photography: Robert Benson

The new living room, far left, sits over the stepped-out garage. By supporting the central steel ceiling beam with a fat column similar to the one found in front of the house, the owners were able to open up the whole first floor.

The kitchen, above, was expanded into a former eat-in area and now flows through to the new formal dining area.

The architect/owner laid out a garden hose to help in the design of the banister's graceful volute or spiral, left, at the bottom of the main staircase. On the far side of the banister, another set of stairs leads to the basement.

Southern
Exposure

Removing the carport-like overhang, inset, a Northern architect
designed a proper front porch for a Southern client, transforming
both the exterior style and the feeling inside the house.

obin McGary grew up in the South on front porches and in sunlight-flooded rooms. Marrying and moving North, however, she found herself in a pale imitation of those early houses—a kind of Colonial Raised Ranch (so-called because there is one level in the front and two in the back), built extensively in the '60s in this New England suburb, with a shallow, carport-like portico and small, dark rooms. An interior designer, Robin began redesigning the interior, combining the living room and dining room under a cathedral ceiling, while her architect, Joseph Matto, transformed the exterior.

The challenge, as the architect perceived it, was straightforward: "How can we take this house and make it look better?" He started by bringing the portico out another five feet, eliminating a column and a bay, and centering a high gable over the new front porch. Then he set windows into the gable eave, which is also the

top of the living room wall. "Often with cathedral ceilings," Joe says, "the upper volume is very dark. Now, even in winter, sun can penetrate the deepest recesses of the room." The three stock gable windows—a full and two halves—repeat the trio of porch bays below and are much less expensive than the typically used elliptical or half-round windows.

Robin got her front porch and sunlight, but not without concessions to the Union. "I was used to dealing with brick and wrought iron," she says, "but Joe would say, 'Robin, we don't do that up here.' It was like the North against the South between us. I wound up relying on him." Joe finished the redesign by siding the house in clapboard, adding shutters and casing the trim around windows, in keeping with other Colonials on the street.

"Robin said she wanted something that looked more New Orleans," the architect recalls. "I never really understood what she meant. What we ended up with is more reminiscent of a Greek Revival façade that downplays the rest of the house."

The redesigned living room, above, is flooded with light from the front porch. Left, a stairwell niche, a standard feature of many Raised Ranches, finds purpose in a new bathroom.

Photography: Joseph Matto

Upscaled
Contemporary

Strictly speaking, this house doesn't belong in a section called Ranches. It's a shed-style Contemporary, before and after, and probably always will be. But the original had Raised Ranch elements; these houses began popping up in suburban developments in the late 1960s and early '70s; and it's a fine example of how a modest house can be transformed into a magnificent one.

The couple that built the original house in the mid-'80s is the same couple who hired Anthony Terry to expand and update it a decade later. They had more children by the mid-'90s, and a bigger house budget. Given free reign, Tony would have completely changed the style and look of the house. "It was a misplaced piece of construction," he recalls. "It looked like it belonged in Southern California. It was more like driving up to a garage than a house." But the owners liked the basic style, and by the end of the project, so did the architect.

Beginning with the section of the house the couple most wanted to change, Tony converted the existing garage into a Great Room, adding a new roof with skylights parallel to the old one, clerestory windows under the upper eave, and a massive fireplace that demarcates old and new. The entry was moved from the left side of the house to the right, just beyond the chimney. The former front door now leads to a stone terrace, while the new entry opens into a 2,200-square-foot addition: a new kitchen, breakfast area, and guest room on the first floor, and a master-bedroom suite on the second. Children's bedrooms and play area are over the new garage at the far right side of the house.

The new house is nearly double the size of the original, inset, and richer by far in materials, windows, and detail.

Rather than being limited by the original house's roof ridges and slopes, all of which exist on the same planes, Tony created a sense of drama and heightened expectation by varying their dimensions and relationships with one another. He also extensively upgraded the materials used throughout the expanded house. V-groove cedar boards replaced the mix of vertical and diagonal siding. Existing eaves and rakes were extended, emphasizing the roof lines. A wealth of upscale elements —cherry moldings and paneling, granite and cut stone, new windows and skylights—give the entire house a custom-made look.

The 1995 addition and renovation, which increased the size of the structure by more than a third, cost about $200 a square foot.

The repositioned entryway, near right, features a curved wall of glass blocks and cherry paneling; it winds around to the Great Room—a glorified family room. Below, the expanded kitchen flows into a breakfast area and Great Room, beyond.

*The custom front door, upper left, is made of cherry and inset with
squares of glass; it opens into a two-story hallway. Steps off the hall,
lower left, lead to a second-level bridge connecting parents' and chil-
drens' rooms. The light-flooded Great Room, above, was once a garage.*

Ranch of Seven Gables

Architect Mark Finlay took one look at this '60s Connecticut Ranch and said, "Off with the roof!" Known nationally for designing traditional luxury homes of 10,000 square feet and up, Mark agreed to survey the house after three other architects called in to do a redesign had come up with plans that only made it "ranchier." Although Pat and Jeff Scanlan had raised three children in the Ranch, what they really loved were classic Colonials—the kind of house that, on the same acre-and-a-half site, they couldn't afford. Hence the decision to stay put and remodel.

Once the low-pitched, straight lines of the roof were gone, the couple's imagination seemed free to soar. Everywhere in the house the couple enjoyed being, the architect went up by raising ceilings and creating gables and additional space.

An existing gable in the front of the house was extended and pitched more steeply, picking up seven hundred additional square feet in the master bedroom. A screened porch on the opposite side was brought out five feet and turned into a formal dining room under another steeply gabled roof. And the front entrance, formerly a plain door with a carport-like overhang, was dramatically defined by a boxed gable, hefty columns, and wide, stone steps.

After ten years and three children in this '60s' Ranch, inset, the owners' love of Colonial-period style and details finally triumphed.

Possibly the most dramatic changes can be found in the small, cosmetic touches that the original house completely lacked: French doors, thick exterior moldings, old-style lattice work, Chippendale railings. "I love details—I'm a moldings freak," says Pat. "Mark went full-blast with moldings in front of the house, particularly around the entrance. They help to create the look of a stately house."

The total cost of renovation, completed in 1994, was close to what the couple paid for the house ten years earlier.

Chippendale-style railings on back, left, and side balconies, above, complete the transformation of the house from ordinary to classic.

Collector's

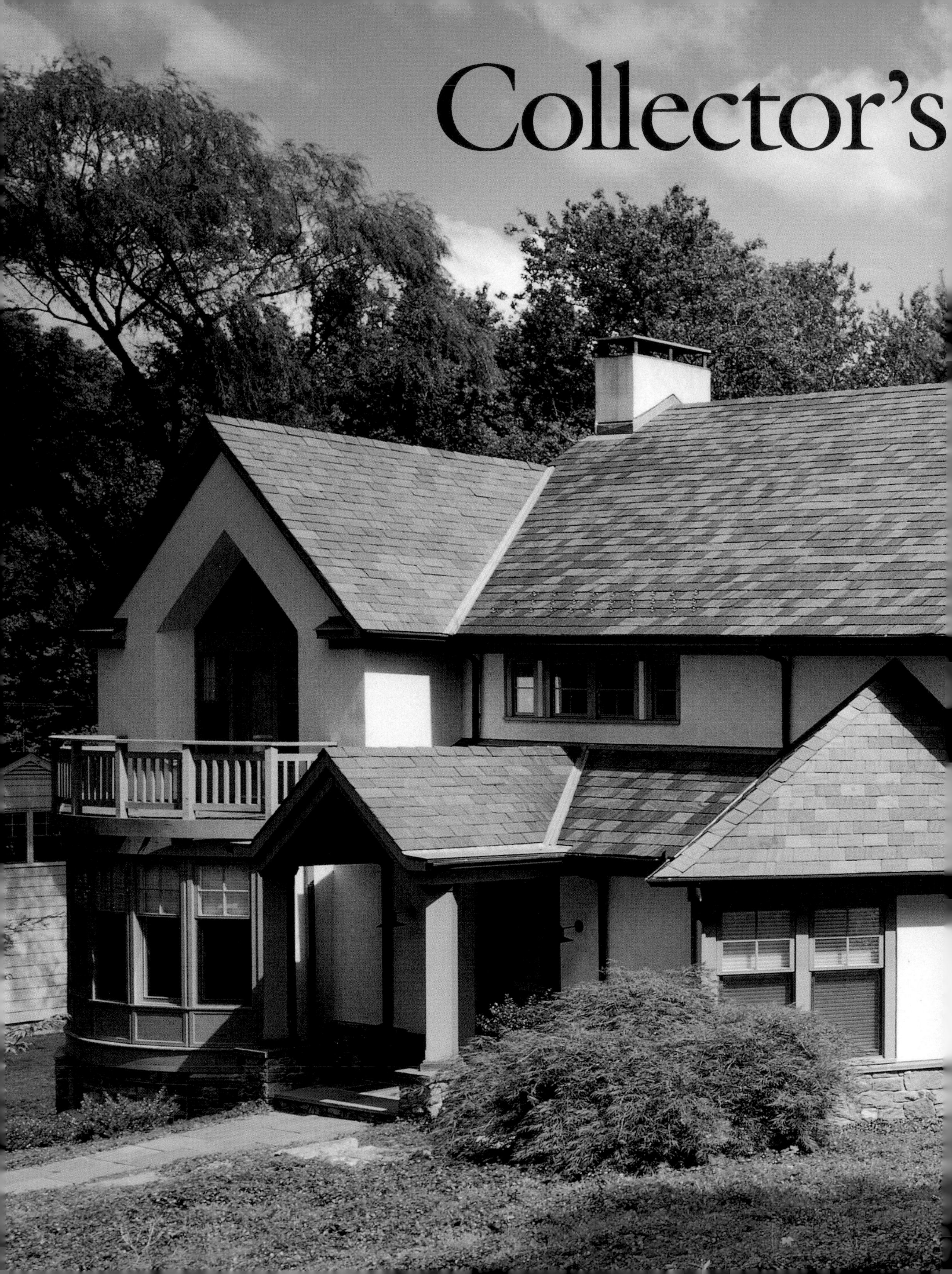

Contemporary

Despite nearly doubling in size, this expanded and transformed '60s Ranch was designed for maximum sunlight and privacy.

Most ranches have nowhere to go but up, and in this case, that coincided with a pressing need of the owners: They are tall—he's 6'7," she's 6'1"—and with one tall child; so they needed more head room. But the main reason for expanding and upscaling the 1960s Ranch was to create a home that would showcase the couple's growing collection of artwork and fine crafts. And while they were at it, they decided to add a few other items to their wish list: a large family room; a gourmet kitchen integrated into dining and informal living areas; and unusually shaped rooms with interesting wall textures, doors, and hardware.

Using the existing foundation and floor platform, architect Rob Sanders created a two-story, custom-fit, collectors' Contemporary from the modest one-story building. In front, to the left of an entrance and doorway of Japanese and Arts and Crafts sensibilities, is a spacious office and study behind a large, curving bay window with balcony above. At the other side of the front door is a polygonal, two-story family room that flows through the interior to the new, extended kitchen and rear dining room, and beyond the family room to a gabled sitting wing. Four bedrooms take up the second floor, including a master bedroom with balconied terrace over the breakfast area.

Custom kitchen cabinets, above left, are cherry and the walls throughout the house tinted plaster. The flooring is inlaid oak in the entrance hall, above right, and tile, slate, and marble elsewhere.

Perhaps most interesting is how the the floor plan aligned most of the living spaces on the property's private, southern side, providing indirect sunlight from morning to late afternoon. That light plays off walls of tinted plaster over sheetrock, while posing no threat to the artwork on display. The doors are Arizona piñon pine; the floors inlaid oak, tile, slate, and marble. And the ceilings—remember the owners' heights?—are a minimum of 8'6".

Outside, the stucco finish and slate roof give the house a massing that suits its rocky site. "The overall shape of the house feels massive," the architect notes. "That was a response to the rock outcropping on the property, and an attempt to take the site and bring it into the house. The slate roof is the finishing touch. It ties it all together."

The conversion, which expanded the square footage from 2,800 to just under 5,000, cost about what the owners paid for the existing house did in 1995.

Rural Villa

N o one is really sure what style this used to be, but everyone agreed it was one of the ugliest houses they had ever seen. "I don't know who built it," notes Skip Broome, the builder, "but it was really ugly." "It was about as bad as you get—it just had this hideous envelope," recalls Brian Lewis, a friend of the owner and an architect in San Antonio, Texas. "Nobody could believe I bought it," adds Sue Cutler, the owner. "This is what tornadoes hit in Florida."

When Sue moved to New York City from Texas a few years ago, another friend of hers, the writer Dominick Dunne, suggested that she find a weekend home near his in northeastern Connecticut. Like other owners of houses in this book, Sue was lured by the land: sixteen high acres overlooking the Connecticut River. The real-estate brochure about the property called the house "French eclectic," but in reality it was a '60s Raised Ranch with metal-frame windows, a speckled red-and-white brick façade, and a TV satellite dish on top of the hip roof.

Carpenters on the job chose to call this transformation of an eclectic Ranch "The Alamo," but it's really closer in style and spirit to an exotic villa.

The expanded and completely refurbished interior, left and below, vanquishes any suggestion of "ranchness."

Right, a nautilus-like staircase leads to the owner's private second-floor apartment within the house.

Sketching ideas on a piece of toilet paper, Brian came up with a redesign that solved the ugly issue and gave the owner the space she required. "Sue wanted a new master bedroom, that's all," he says. "Essentially, we just put a house on top of a house and created an 1,800-square-foot, second-floor apartment for her." To get Sue into the house before the snows, Skip Broome's crew cut holes in the existing roof and built the second floor and new roof, then took out the old ceiling and roof.

After jackhammering the old brick and the windows, the contractor reframed the house and stuccoed the exterior, setting

The central addition, left, rises above the remodeled wings and pool to take advantage of spectacular views of the Connecticut River in the distance.

blocks of limestone into the façade. He installed a limestone floor in the entry hall and a spiral staircase. The wrought-iron balconies in the front and back are custom-made.

The two-story center section completely changes the proportion and focus of the house, not to mention the look. Now, although Skip's crew likes to refer to it as "The Alamo," no one's really sure what to call the new house, and it no longer really matters.

Photography: Robert Benson

House on the Edge

Transformation may be too meek a word for what happened to this unprepossessing, cottage-like Ranch north of Chicago. Transmutation may be closer to the bone.

The owners, a contractor and his wife, bought the late-'30s/early-'40s house with the intention of having Doug Garofalo, the Chicago architect, design a new home for them. "They said they wanted 'Contemporary' and something sculptural," he recalls, "and that they liked an edgy, angled design." Doug, as it turns out, does "angled." He does "edgy." Nevertheless, he more than had his work cut out for him.

New owners of this midwestern Ranch, inset, wanted something "sculptural" and "edgy." Architect Doug Garofalo delivered.

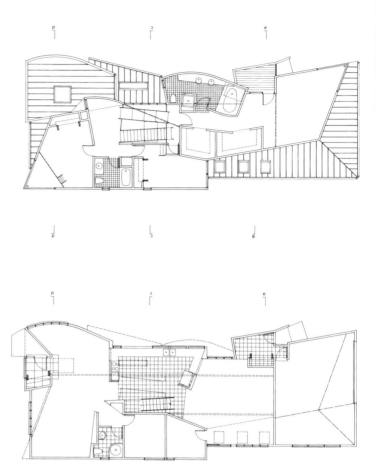

At the end of a cross-hatched brick walk, the new front entrance, right, cuts sharply away from the lot's tight property lines

A convex wall of standing-seam steel houses the central staircase, above. The architect's renderings could easily be adapted to a future development in Roswell, New Mexico.

The house was unusually sited on the small lot, hard by property lines on two sides so that only a 40' by 80' section of yard was left unoccupied. Assisted by two designers in his office, Ellen Grimes and Minkyu Whang, Doug took a variety of shapes—squares and odd rectangles, curves and acute angles—and devised a façade that interlocked these elements in an attempt to organize and maximize the limited exterior space. "The last thing we wanted was a big, pretentious façade that would overpower the yard," he says. "The forms create multiple faces to what is the owners' only yard. They're meant to be animated against that very beautiful backdrop."

To the right of the front entrance are two sharp wedges of rooms: the living room on the first level, and a child's bedroom with a large, triangulated window on the second. Around the back door, the kitchen is to the right, behind a narrow band of windows. To the left is the rear entry foyer and above it the master bedroom and deck. The master bath lays hidden behind a large, curved sheet of standing-seam steel.

Painted in muted tones, as if to camouflage its existence among the spruce trees and lawn, it is settling into the neighborhood, although the neighborhood may never be the same again.

California Modern

San Francisco architects Steven and Cathi House design distinctive homes and additions. The couple who contacted them knew their work, knew architecture, collected Corbusier and Macintosh furniture, and said they wanted to expand and renovate in a way that was bold and original. For ten years they had lived in a 1940s house that, at best, was a nondescript Ranch wishing to be something grander. But during that time their family had grown significantly, and so had their tastes. And if only in California could one find a ranch with Tudor aspirations, then perhaps only there could an addition to it become what House + House Architects wound up designing.

Since Steven and Cathi knew that the local design-review board was certain to deny any changes to the façade, they used the exist-

Hidden from the street by the existing house—
a nondescript 1940s Ranch with Tudor-aspira-
tions—this brave new wing takes fabulous flight.

The old living room, inset, has been replaced by a long, modern room with free-standing fireplace and irregular windows. The windows in the new entry, near right, diffuse the strong Western sunlight while blocking out views of the houses next door. In the master bathroom, far right, surround-sound is built into the ceiling above the modern shower.

Like other rooms in the 2,700-square-foot addition, the new kitchen is both more spacious and elegant than the old, inset, right. Stained Douglas fir cabinets and floor contrast with black-granite counter tops, which almost seem to disappear. Elsewhere in the wing the floors are Cantera stone.

The former rear and flank of the house, inset, was renovated to accommodate the modern wing.

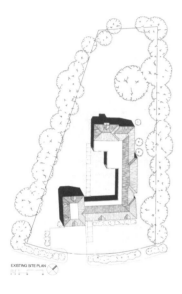

EXISTING SITE PLAN

From the courtyard formed between the old and new structures, daily life has also been totally transformed.

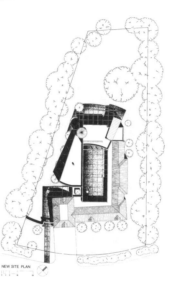

NEW SITE PLAN

ing 2,700-square-foot ranch as a "front" for a modern, wedge-shaped, stuccoed addition that is hidden from the street and is as bold and original as the existing Ranch was ordinary.

Influenced by the work of Mexican architect Luis Barragan, the new wing plays off archetypal building forms—cylinders, cubes, wedges, and cones—that are skinned with cement plaster in shades of rose and lavender. The addition doubled the size of the house and serves as new living, dining, kitchen, family, and master bedroom space. It also encloses a new courtyard that functions both as a central outdoor room and as a source of light and air. The small squares of glass and long, narrow windows temper the strong Western sun and diffuse the light entering the house. The old house, which was gutted and renovated, contains bedrooms for the couple's four children, plus a family room and maid's room.

Although the original '40s' Ranch passes as the primary residence, the eye and mind are immediately pulled around to the left side of the house through a ceremonial gate and into the new formal entrance between the house and new wing. From this vantage point, family life is being lived in the twenty-first century.

Like Capes, Colonials are probably the most ubiquitous residential form built in America in the twentieth century. From an interest in Colonial Revivalism late in the nineteenth century to the spread of small, economical Colonials during the Depression, the style developed into a suburban formula that was simple to build, familiar and comforting to imagine living in, and relatively inexpensive to buy.

While the earliest examples in New England possessed a Puritanical spareness and restraint of detail, in the eighteenth century they became larger and increasingly more elaborate. During the 1980s, in fact, Colonials constructed in developments in some parts of the country had grown into what architects Bruce Beinfield and Jonathan Wagner termed "Contempalonials." Today, the style provides "a kind of license," says Patrick Pinnell, an architect and former visiting professor at the Yale School of Architecture, "either to ornament or leave spare."

Many of the Builders' Colonials shown here do both. Some owners have upgraded the façades; others have added front porches, instantly converting the houses to Farmhouse Colonials.

Most have left the houses unaltered in front, presenting a spare, simple face to the other Colonials on the street, while going wild behind the houses with glassy, two-story, open-vista additions: family rooms, Great Rooms, sun rooms, space-and-light rooms.

BUILDERS'
COLONIALS

Formal Entrance

Nothing was really standard in this 1960 Garrison Colonial (modeled after early, fort-like New England houses in which the second story projected beyond the first). The original owner, George Grenadier, founded The Grenadier Corporation, a masonry restoration and waterproofing company in New York City with a reputation for integrity and high craftsmanship. That level of work went into George and Del Grenadier's home as well: The roof is thick slate, the brickwork around the house superbly set, the floors made with the best tile and hardwood.

But like many other late-twentieth century Colonials in the suburbs, their house lacked a front entrance substantial or gracious enough to bring guests properly into the beautiful interior. When George and Del died within a year of one another not long ago, James Ezzes, a Westport, Connecticut, contractor, bought the house and began updating it.

While workmen opened up the rooms, and expanded and modernized the kitchen, others removed the existing front steps and in their place erected a spacious brick and slate porch. Double width sidelights were installed on either side of the door and a flat-roofed portico, supported by slender Doric columns and topped by a wood balustrade, was built out five feet from the façade. "The new entrance gives the house a focal point it didn't have before," says Ezzes. The balustrade also helps bring balance to the long, horizontal line of the front of the house. "Other classic Colonials around town don't have balustrades," the contractor notes, "but this is now a classic Colonial."

Work continues inside the house, but the front entrance was finished first at a cost of around $8,000.

This 1960 Garrison Colonial was always gracious but lacked an entrance commensurate with the owners' taste and hospitality.

Custom Cottage

Developers built Builders' Colonials long before World War II, and this was one of them: a 1920s' two-story rectangle with fake gambrel roof and second-floor shed dormer to simulate the Dutch Colonial style. "The Dutch Colonial was a style and trend of the day, I suppose," says Paul Harris, an industrial designer who redesigned the house. "This was an affordable way to copy it."

The designer's clients had sold a builder's spec home in the same town in order to be on the water; their new house backs up to a shimmering cove on the southern New England coast. But here, as in other examples in this book, the views were cut off by small windows in small rooms; the house could have been anywhere. And so, in the process of expanding the seventy-year-old structure for a modern family of four, Paul renovated the rooms that worked, but completely altered the rest of the house, opening it up to the site. "We found there was value to the structure and the location of some rooms," he says. "We chose to leave all the existing bedrooms on the first floor in place, and get the biggest bang for the buck by expanding the kitchen and building a new family room off the back."

The transformation begins at the front entrance. While the old door was off center (located under the oval to the left of the new door), the new entrance is in the exact center of the house. It is announced by the generous curve in the porch roof, which also

The redesigned façade of this 1920s' Builders' Colonial announces its charm, custom woodwork, and individuality to the neighborhood.

The crowded kitchen, inset, expanded to meet the family's needs. The interior columns carry that element from the front of the house to the back.

breaks up the linearity of the front of the house, and by the solidity of the thick columns. In the open doorway, the curve funnels the light off the water that streams straight through the center hall from the back of the house. "It's important that when you come to the front door you know you're on the water," notes the designer. To further the effect, he sheathed the hall ceiling in beadboard, then painted it to catch the light reflected from the cove. He also foreshortened the second-floor windows and brought the new porch roof up to meet them, minimizing the shed-dormer effect. "The whole push," he says, "was to make this look like a small, shingle cottage on the water."

On the back side of the house, new gables with five-foot-high oval windows maximize the view: The oval on the right looks out from a loft in the new master bedroom; the left oval occupies most of the outer wall of a small office. Off the family room, a porch extends in a semicircle out over the lawn, allowing the master bedroom deck above to do the same and providing a sweeping, second-floor view of the cove.

Open for viewing: ground-floor French doors, a second-floor balcony off the master bedroom, and five-foot-high oval windows in an upper loft and office bring the water up to the house.

Seaside Colonial

This little Gambrel Colonial sits nestled in an early development of seventeen summer houses, loosely styled after American seaside architecture and built on a narrow spit of sand between a mill pond and Long Island Sound on the East coast. Its current owner would have been far better off tearing the place down and starting over; there was no heat or insulation, the foundation was shaky, and erosion necessitated moving the house farther back from the beach. But since zoning doesn't permit tear-downs here, and since the site is so pristinely beautiful, the only thing to do was to renovate and, while he was at it, redesign.

After the house was jacked up and repositioned and the foundation shored, Stuart Disston of Austin, Patterson, Disston architects in Southport, Connecticut, brought the façade out another twelve feet, creating space for a mudroom, a two-story music

Rather than hide this small Colonial's Gambrel lineage, the renovated house celebrates it, while framing and presenting a more welcoming entrance.

Light off the water, and a spare and simple style inspired by life on the beach, rule the new interior.

room, and a second-floor study, and doubling the size of the house to just under 2,000 square feet. A double-gambrel roof was built to balance the asymmetry of the original façade. The new roof updates the house and frames the open sky and sea beyond, while the bowed ridge between the large gables anchors the front door and serves as a nautical reference. The architect also added a wide, sheltered entrance and a cozy deck off the master bedroom on the waterside of the house. The entire exterior was re-sided with gray wood shingles.

Inside, the original walls of exterior plywood and studs were replaced with horizontal boards, but the rafters were left exposed in keeping with a shore house. All of the rooms have the spare, simple, fresh feel of life lived on the water, an effect Stuart created by opening the rooms so that they flow into one another, installing French doors and sidelights in the rear wall, and giving every room in the house a view of the water.

The extensive renovation added up to roughly the cost of the house in 1996.

Right, the renovated house looks pretty much the same to passing beachcombers and boats, but now the owner has better views, including that from the master bedroom balcony, upper right.

Photography: Jeff McNamara

Establishment Colonial

Builders' Colonials are so adaptable that most of the time a change of siding and a redesigned entrance can transform a house's character and style. Which is exactly what the owners of this brick-faced Garrison Colonial wanted and got.

Three walls of windows and a skylighted ceiling transformed a screened porch, inset, into a year-round sunroom.

T he couple had lived in the place for fifteen years before realizing that the houses they really liked were the older Colonials dotting their town. Not wanting to leave their street or well-cultivated gardens, they asked Christopher Carpiniello to "make the house special," the architect recalls. "We sought to mask completely what this house was and make it appear to be a stately home that's been here for some time."

The first things to go were the brick veneer and asphalt shingle siding—typical '60s development touches. They were replaced with wood shingles, giving the façade what Chris calls "an instant established look." Leafing through books on New England architecture and looking at porticos in the area, he came up with a Georgian-style entrance and overhang based on those found in finer old homes. Copper covers the barrel-shaped roof of the portico; underneath is a beadboard ceiling and thick Doric columns. "We fattened them up a little," notes the architect, "because we think it makes the front of the house look a little more powerful."

At the back of the house, a screened porch was taken down and in its place a flat-roofed sunroom was erected; skylights, hidden from view, let in even more sky and sun. Also in back is a second addition with a flat roof, which the owners use as a music room. On top of the garage, meanwhile, the architect set a small cupola inspired by the kind he'd seen on New England barns. This custom-made, trapezoidal element—"It's a little more special than what you'd find at Home Depot," he points out—opens up the room above the garage while extending and projecting the old Colonial image.

Luxuriating in the privacy of a shielded backyard, the sunroom, below, is free to be more Classical Revival than Colonial. The railing above the room hides the skylights.

Photography: Dan Cornish

It's all in the details: Gabled portico, fanlight window, columns and capitals, ornamental post finials, window cornices and cedar-shake roof help turn a run-of-the-mill Builders' Colonial from the 1970s into a timeless home.

Georgian Details

The developer seems to have had a general idea of the Colonial style when he built this spec house in a subdivision of beautiful lots in northern Connecticut in the late 1970s. But that is as far as he went. The house was basically a two-story rectangle in front and a hodgepodge of gables and roof lines in the rear. There were no details, no charm, and no real character.

"That was fine when we were first married," says the wife, who with her husband bought the house on three acres in the early '80s. "But as you grow and change, your tastes change. We began to miss having nooks and crannies, and wonderful doorways, and crown moldings." Working with local contractors and later with Bob Harper of Robert Harper Architects in Centerbrook, Connecticut, the couple first made some practice changes on the back of the house.

Expanding the kitchen and opening up the entire rear with gables, they added lots of glass and a ten-foot extension off the roof that's supported by Tuscan columns and covers a summer outdoor cooking and entertaining area. From this view, in fact, the house looks more like a villa in the Italian countryside than a contemporary Colonial in New England. The experience in transforming the back of the house proved invaluable, as it turned out, in planning changes to the front. "We got to know the house," the husband recalls, "and we got to know ourselves."

Out front, the couple formalized and Georgified the main entrance using the kinds of classical elements—pedimented columns, a fanlight window above the door, posts with pineapple finials at the beginning of the front walk—they had long admired. Where a flat, unsheltered door used to bring visitors immediately into the house, a gabled overhang, fat columns, and wide, floor-to-fascia

board windows enclose a generous exterior vestibule that's far more welcoming, as well as attractive. "Now the house has a great deal of elegance," says the husband, "but it's also inviting. And that is more us than the old house was." The cost: "Three times more than I expected," he confesses.

The new entry is more than a redesigned front door. It is also a focal point of the renovated house and an exterior room that shelters visitors from the elements.

Behind the neighborhood's back, a Colonial can be whatever it wants to be. Here, the plain rear façade with a jumble of rooflines has taken on the look and feel of a classic summer villa. The back of the garage, usually a blank wall, is extended and given expression by means of a one-sided, attached pergola.

Photography: Robert Benson

English Sunroom

Many owners of Builders' Colonials like the way their houses look and wouldn't change a thing, at least not out front. Yet nearly all of the homeowners in this book shared a common dream and goal — to open up small rooms, create bigger family spaces, and bring broad views and full light into once-dark interiors . And for most of them, including this couple, the back of the house is ideal for such dreams and transformations.

Here, architect Robert Orr took a plain, unornamented Builders' Colonial in Connecticut and added a rear sunroom inspired by John Nash (1752–1835), the English architect noted for opulent Georgian homes (he redesigned Buckingham Palace) and solariums. These two almost opposing styles produced in Connecticut this addition, that is somewhere in the middle. "The house had very simple materials and detailing, so we didn't want to do the John Nash thing full-blown," says Orr. "We tried to make a kind of crude interpretation that would fit into the American Colonial vernacular. We were aiming toward Georgian but through the eyes of a Colonial builder."

The sixteen by twenty-four foot room more than makes up for the architectural details the rest of the house lacks without calling too much attention to itself. In the recessed triangular eave (or

The "before" of this Builders' Colonial can be seen behind the new formal addition. Inspired by British architect John Nash, the room opens the back of the house to the land and light.

A most un-Colonial-like room, the addition's elaborate interior features ten-inch crown molding assemblies, paneling, niches and antique pine flooring. Through French doors; a terrace, pool and shingle-style poolhouse with dressing rooms, kitchen, laundry, bath and sauna.

tympanum) above the French doors is a custom-made "wheel" window inspired by a Nash solarium in London. Unfluted Doric columns with extended entablature rise to meet the rake returns. The terrace was designed by Orr's wife, landscape-designer Carol Chamberlain. Inside, builder Skip Broom turned an existing fireplace ninety degrees so it faces the new room. In his shop he custom-milled and installed assemblies of crown moldings that define the gabled ceiling and the ornate niches along the interior walls. The wide antique-pine flooring was stained and stenciled.

When one arrives here at the end of a placid walk through the rest of the Colonial, notes Orr, "this room blossoms into a sensational space that is the pièce-de-resistance of the entire house."

Revolutionary Remodel

One of the first building booms in this country came during and following the Revolutionary War, when a war-time economy allowed people to expand their dwellings. Colonial-era houses were designed to be added to, after all. Yet no one, no matter how prosperous or forward-thinking, could have envisioned this late-twentieth-century expansion and transformation.

Built before the Revolution by Hezekiah Ripley, a chaplain in Washington's army, the house was burned nearly to the ground during a raid in 1779, then rebuilt and added onto many times over the centuries. By the time a young couple bought the old house a few years ago, some of the original oak beams were being held in place by little more than the plaster walls above them. The first three architects called in saw nothing worth saving. The fourth firm, however—A.D. Ialeggio Associates, run by Anthony Ialeggio and Elizabeth Einiger—perceived what the owner felt. "I found the history of the house so compelling, I just couldn't bring myself to level it ," the wife says. "I knew we could restore it, and so did Tony and Elizabeth."

The architects salvaged the best of the early structure and designed the twenty-first-century renovation and addition around that. The front gable with exposed roof rafters is original, as is the location of the front door, although the doorway itself is new. The carved pineapple above the door is a sym-

The former kitchen, inset, was a good place to be alone sometimes. Now it's the center of family activity.

*On the sunny side of the street: The renovated house, with
new side decks and playroom above a three-car garage,
makes the most of its southern exposure.*

bol of hospitality, and the "broken bonnet" pediment an early
Colonial detail. Shed additions to either side of the house were
removed and new areas seamlessly adjoined. The narrow, two-
story, gabled projection on the far right gathers additional space
and light for a living room with terrace on the first floor and a
master bedroom suite on the second. Including a new, three-car
garage with a children's playroom above, the area of the house
expanded from 2,800 to just under 6,000 square feet.

Inside the house, a broad center hall runs from front to back,
linking original, small rooms with seven-foot ceilings to new,
communal, high-ceilinged areas. A number of cramped rooms
were combined to create the completely remodeled kitchen,
which opens onto the hallway, a seating area flanked by bookcas-
es, a breakfast room, and a sunken TV room with deck. Susan
Albright of Susan Albright Design Inc. picked out moldings,
hardware, lighting, and built-ins. Throughout the house the
architects left exposed the 200-year-old posts and beams that
reveal the house's true, unalterable character.

The additions and renovation cost about two times the price of
the house in 1997.

Un-
Garrison
Addition

If the original Ranch "Modern" in the previous section might have been home to "The Brady Bunch," this 1950s' Garrison Colonial could have been the setting for "Ozzie & Harriet." Life, as viewed from the front of the house at least, looked perfect— white clapboard, green shutters and trim, not a shrub out of place — and perfectly in keeping with the rest of the relatively high-end Rhode Island neighborhood.

But the rear of the house was a different story. Despite several previous renovations, the exterior continued to have problems relating to the well-maintained landscape and terrace and pool. Inside, the rear rooms were small and dark. The owners wanted more space and light, but this time around they wanted it to be quality space and all the light the northern exposure could provide.

Rich in architectural detail, a multidimensional addition transforms the back of an otherwise undistinguished '50s Garrison Colonial.

Newport, Rhode Island architect James Estes and contractor Matt Davitt came up with a six-foot addition that runs the length of the back of house and includes an entry porch and mudroom and an expanded kitchen and dining room with elevated ceilings. At the same time, Jim bumped out the family room an additional twelve feet under a barrel-shaped roof with walls of Colonial-style windows and French doors. The addition incorporates and accentuates the existing terrace and pool. The architect also added exterior detail too fancy perhaps for the front of the house: an elliptical window in the family room gable, lower panel walls, pilasters (shallow, attached columns) with heavily molded bases, and copper carriage lanterns.

From the street, life goes on as it has for nearly half a century. But now from the rear of the house, this Garrison Colonial looks inviting rather than impenetrable, and as romantic as an English country house.

A new porched entry, above left, leads to a mudroom and bathroom. Below left, the addition's vaulted ceiling reflects light from the custom-milled elliptical window.

Expanding the kitchen, below, made room for an island, walls of cabinets, and full views of the backyard.

Photography: Aaron Usher

Farmhouse Colonial

Gables, rake returns and an old-fashioned porch give

this expanded '70s Garrison Colonial the look and

feel of a classic New England farmhouse.

For a couple whose lives center around their four young children, this house was practically ideal. A 2,400-square-foot Garrison Colonial in the middle of a '70s development of nearly identical houses, it had generous rooms and a big backyard. That was the practical aspect. Aesthetically, there wasn't much to it. "They were efficient houses for the money and obviously filled the bill for people at the time," says Jeff Rowe of Stratfield Builders, the contractor for what was to come. "The developer scrimped where he could. In the '70s, there were no overhangs and the exterior trim got smaller and smaller."

The husband and wife had both grown up in the same Connecticut town and both loved old houses, but they loved this neighborhood of young families more. They hired Jeff, a long-time friend, to make the place into a house they could love, too. After taking down the original garage and an addition, both of which were in bad shape, he built a new two-bay garage on a slightly larger footprint. This allowed for a mudroom, bathroom, and laundry behind the garage, and a large master bedroom above, with room for a back staircase from the bedroom to the garage.

Front porches are perfect places for
four-year-old girls like Margo, above.

Left, this multifaceted rear exterior is far more interesting
than the original, inset, and more functional: from left to
right, the new back entry, family room, and screened porch.

He also built a front porch with railing and lattice; it's an old, Colonial farmhouse look as well as a way to draw visitors to the front door, which previously saw little use. Behind the house, where the family spends much of its time, the contractor built a twenty by twenty-four foot family room off one end and a screened porch off the other. Between the two rooms is a semi-enclosed patio and a three-foot-wide extended roof, which overhangs the kitchen window and ties the additions together.

The most distinctive things about this transformation are its subtlety and balance. The new house is one-third larger than the original, but you'd hardly know it. At both ends of the house, front and back, the gable forms and the returns at the bottoms of the rakes give the place a sense of scale and continuity seldom seen in renovated development homes. "I think we almost obliterated the character of the Builders' Colonial," Jeff concludes. "It's a different house; it really reflects the owners and the type of life they envision for themselves. It's still a Colonial; it just doesn't look like a spec house anymore—it looks like a house that was designed and built with care."

Added off the living room, a twenty by twenty-four foot
family room employs French doors and transoms to take
advantage of the spacious backyard and woods beyond.

Great Room

The owners of this '50s house had done Colonial. They'd done Traditional. They'd raised children here and lived in perfect symmetry with the other Builders' Colonials on the quiet street in Princeton, New Jersey. Now it was time for something completely different.

In practical terms, the couple wanted a big room for listening to music and enjoying the grounds, so they called in architect Michael Fairwell. "The house had a beautiful garden, but because these builder houses are formulaic, because the prototypes are standard forms, it had been closed off to the landscape," he observes. "They were willing to experiment with the addition and have it contrast with the house. The key thing was to have the rectangle stand on its own and let the new wing be its own piece."

It's own building: A new wing off a '50s Colonial, inset, takes its cues not from the main house but from the garden and the muses.

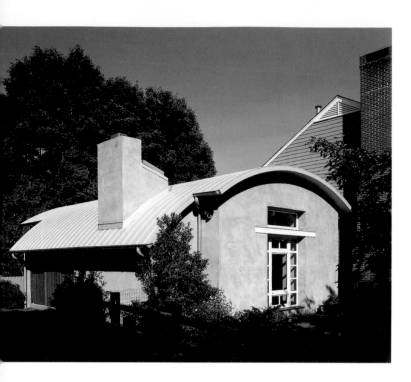

Michael came up with an asymmetrical, domed addition, eighteen feet at its widest point and forty feet long—a "Great Room"—that doubles as an entertainment wing and a garden solarium. A grand piano, showcased in a large, boxed window, fills the front of the room; a modern fireplace warms the back. But along its south-eastern face is a glazed wall with an upper clerestory devoted to viewing the broad back terrace and gardens. Further enhancing the effect, a section of this wall juts out at an angle behind the house, and through a pyramid-shaped skylight that sits on the extension like a wizard's cap, captures more of the sun.

While the Great Room feels like a contemporary vacation home, it's clearly related to the main house. The wide-ribbed stucco façade, painted in the same shade of gray, echoes the Colonial's narrower clapboards. The addition was part of a large renovation project that also included a new kitchen.

Restrained and muted in front like the parent house, the wing blossoms behind a full wall of garden views and southeastern light.

In spite of its original size, this Colonial from the late '40s had no single room in which to entertain the new owners' many friends.

Colonial Conservatory

Big doesn't necessarily mean nice, and custom doesn't necessarily mean detailed, as this 3,000-square-foot Colonial from the late '40s attested. "There was nothing really special about it," says David Preusch, the architect hired at the end of the 1990s to redesign the house. "It had a terrible plan with a very small entertaining area, and very little exterior detail. It was just shingles and windows."

The new owner and his wife, who love to entertain, wanted to expand the living room and master bedroom off the back of the house, as well as enlarge an existing porch at the side. When the architect showed him an option for the porch that included a domed top, however, the focus of the project suddenly changed. Now, instead of a larger living room or porch, the center of attention would be a glass-domed conservatory of classical proportions and exquisite detail.

David had the old porch pulled down and in its place erected a two-story wing containing a new living room on the first level and a master-bedroom suite above. Then he created a hallway to lead from the wing to the new conservatory. Designed along the lines of a Classical Revival pavilion, the twenty-four-square-foot room has a splendid open feeling, with a service bar along one wall and on the other three, under the gables, large windows that are bowed to accommodate seating and circular tables for as many as twenty-four dinner guests. The dome, which was made in England, is lit by fiber optics. New Hampshire artist Susan Pratt Smith painted the transom glass.

While in the process of renovating the rear and right side of the house, the architect also facelifted the façade, adding corner pilasters, rakes, new shutters, and shingles. But the conservatory is clearly the favorite child in the owners' eyes. Looking ahead to their golden years spent under the dome, the room was designed barrier-free for future wheelchair accessibility.

Classically inspired but lit by fiber optics, the conservatory wing is a kind of temple to modern living and entertaining.

Photography: Dan Cornish

21st-Century Colonial

This early '70s Garrison Colonial was a dream house when the young owners, both doctors, had two children. Predictable in design and sufficient in size, it required little thought or imagination. But when a third child was born and the family changed, the house didn't and the dream began turning nightmarish. Not only was there not enough room, but the rooms themselves were proving impractical.

"Predictability isn't always a bad thing," says Duo Dickinson, the Connecticut architect and author. "First-time home buyers would rather have a known entity than deal with idiosyncratic layout. Unfortunately, the family life of most 1990s households is anything but predictable. And when a predictable house has to conform to a customized life, it can't be resolved with decorating and furniture layouts."

When the family grew and changed, this '70s Garrison, inset, was forced to follow. In the process, it became a contemporary, practical home.

Not able to afford a new house, and not willing to leave the town, the couple hired Duo to custom-fit this spec house to their particular family's needs. The husband and wife, both Californians, wanted the renovated space to remind them of West Coast living. They also asked for a new front entrance and a master bedroom suite that would function as a "house-within-a-house." Duo is known for innovative small-house design, but here he went the opposite way.

The architect designed a new, two-story addition that projects from the center of the façade and is faced with a collage of windows, something that might be found in a suburban California home. A new front door under a contemporary overhang picks up

Transplanted Californians, the owners wanted—and got— an addition that reminded them of West Coast living.

An open floor plan allows the family to live, work and play both separately and together.

the addition's roof pitch and gable angle. The addition's first story is a multipurpose family room, open to the kitchen and family dining area; the second story contains a new master bedroom and office with a separate staircase. Duo also designed a smaller projection over the garage to serve as a localized "kid zone."

"None of these features is ever found in any builder spec homes of the '70s," the architect notes. "No home could ever predict the precise recipe that this family called for." The renovation added 2,000 square feet to the house and changed the way the existing space is utilized. Finished in 1989, the renovation cost about what the house itself had nine years earlier.

Enlightened
Colonial

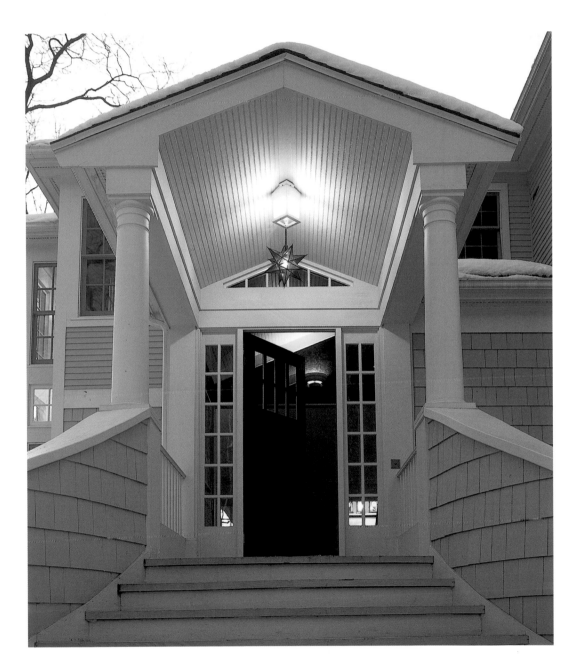

*The new entrance, above, to this transformed 1950s Colonial is as hard to miss as the as the old entrance was
hard to find. Viewed from the rear, left, the house features two-story towers of glass and open space.*

As often happens, the owners of this 1950s Builders' Colonial lived in the house for twenty-five years, raising a family, and building both their careers, before realizing they didn't really like it. "I hated it," corrects the husband, a retired physician, who collects and repairs antique clocks as a hobby. But it took the passing of the old, avocado-colored refrigerator to precipitate the house's total transformation. "When it died, we had to decide whether to fix it or get a new one," he says. "And if we got a new refrigerator, we'd have to redesign the kitchen."

The couple's interior designer, Helen Theurkauf, referred them to Craig Saunders, the architect whose own house appears on page 154. The four of them then set about to address the existing Colonial's "issues."

Foremost on the list was light. Despite its site atop a hill in northeastern Connecticut, the boxy Dutch Colonial was typically dark. The architect vanquished the darkness with two, relatively small, rear additions: a three-story tower and a two-story conservatory. Together they amount to about 800 square feet of new space, extended out of doors by a ship-like deck that wraps around to the front of the house. So effective is the massing of windows in the additions, however, that they appear to double the size of the existing house.

"The verticality, obviously, of the tower multiples the new space by a considerable amount visually," observes the architect. "Also, as you approached the house it always seemed that it was going to come sliding down the hill on top of me. The tower and the curving deck have had the effect of driving a spike into the thing and holding it on the hillside."

The tower also serves as a magnificent display case for the husband's clocks, which he now repairs in the former living room, while his wife, a psychologist, practices the pleasure principle. "It's a pure pleasure," she says, "to live in this house now."

Found objects—the antique fluted column, the etched-glass basement door—grace a hallway off the rear deck, above; the floor is oak and tumbled marble.

In the conservatory, right, light floods a breakfast area off the open kitchen; the floor here is limestone with tumbled marble insets.

Photography: Robert Benson

This telescoped hybrid-Colonial/Cape, inset, appeared to be sliding down the site, literally and figuratively, until it was rescued by a master bedroom/garage addition and a two-story family room in back.

Contemporary Shingle Style

A couple with eyes more for the land than the house, Craig and Ilona Saunders found an acre-and-a-quarter lot, backing up to ten square miles of nature preserve, that happened to be occupied by a Capey Colonial or a Colonial Cape; Craig, an architect, isn't sure which is accurate. Built in stages, with each addition smaller and lower than the preceding one, the second floor of the main section had sloped eaves and low windows. And, like most Capes, the entire house was cramped and dark. The Saunders bought the property in 1988, then waited until 1993 to renovate.

Since their favorite spot was a small awninged patio in back, they started with a soaring, glassed Garden Room that extends seventeen feet from the rear of the house and is seventeen feet high. All of the French doors and tall, double-hung windows open. "In the summer," he says, "you really feel like you're on a porch—we have all that light and we can see up into the trees." In fall and winter, a central fireplace heats the room as well as a small, open, second-level office.

The entire back of the renovated house now responds to the property: terrace, gardens, open lawn, and ten square miles of nature preserve.

The architect left the front of the original sections alone, with the exception of a dormer added to the last one—a single-car garage. Because the three sections appear to be sliding down the property, he designed a new, two-car garage with a master bedroom and bath under a perpendicular, saltbox roof to stop the visual slide. In front, a tall, narrow, projecting bay takes advantage of the southern exposure and appears to anchor the earlier sections. In back, a multiwindowed gable balances the mass and silhouette of the Garden Room addition, while French doors open from the master bedroom to create the essence of a small, private balcony.

Craig deliberately left the new, cedar-shingled wing unpainted. "We wanted to have a clear separation between the new and the old," he explains. "We wanted to be very, very clear about the fact that the house had been extensively modified, but we also wanted to be very respectful of the original house." To the original 1,800-square-feet the couple added another 1,000 square feet at a cost, in 1994, of $130,000.

Sources

Architects, Designers & Builders

CAPES

Edmund Clemente
Beinfield Wagner
1 Marshall Street
South Norwalk, CT 06854
203 838-5789
bwaia@earthlink.net

Robert Sanders
Faesy & Sanders Architects
523 Danbury Road
Wilton, CT 06897
203 834-2724

Mark Hutker & Associates Architects
P.O. Box 2347
Vineyard Haven, MA 02568
508 693-3344
hutker@hutkerarchitects.com

Andrew A. Flake, Inc.
General Contractors
Main Street
Vineyard Haven, MA 02568
508 693-3340

Mark P. Finlay Architects
1300 Post Road
Fairfield, CT 06490
203 254-2388
www.markfinlay.com

James Estes and Company Architects
79 Thames Street
Newport, RI 02840
401 846-3336

Anthony Amenta
Amenta/Emma Architects
201 Ann Street
Hartford, CT 860 549-4725
32 Warren Street
Cambridge, MA 617 492-3662
amenta/emma@aol.com

Harrison Gill
Gill & Gill Architects
39 Wall Street
Norwalk, CT 06850
203 831-8808

Ellen Hyde Phillips
80 Thorpe Street
Fairfield Interiors
Fairfield, CT 06430
203 256-8008

David Raymond
Raymond Design Builders
66 Robson Place
Fairfield, CT 06430
203 256-1246

Donald Richardson AIA
150 Waterman Street
Providence, RI 02906
401 243-9400
dsrich@worldnet.att.net

Douglas Garofalo
Garofalo Architects
3752 North Ashland Avenue
Chicago, IL 60613
773 975-2069
dougg@uic.edu

RANCHES

McKee Patterson
Austin Patterson Disston Architects
376 Pequot Avenue
Southport, CT 06490
203 255-4031

Joseph Matto A.I.A.
37 Geneva Road
Norwalk, CT 06850
203 866-5777

Steven House
House+House AIA Architects
1499 Washington Street
San Francisco, CA 94109
415 474-2112
house@ix.netcom.com

James Childress
Centerbrook Architects and Planners
67 Main Street
Centerbrook, CT 06409
860 767-0175

Anthony Amenta
Amenta/Emma Architects
201 Ann Street
Hartford, CT 860 549-4725
32 Warren Street
Cambridge, MA 617 492-3662
amenta/emma@aol.com

BUILDERS' COLONIALS

Anthony Terry Architects
117 Northford Road
Branford, CT 06405
203 481-6424
architerry@aol.com

Mark P. Finlay Architects
1300 Post Road
Fairfield, CT 06490
203 254-2388
www.markfinlay.com

Robert Sanders
Faesy & Sanders Architects
523 Danbury Road
Wilton, CT 06897
203 834-2724

Skip Broom
H. P. BroomÑHousewright, Inc.
162 Ferry Road
Hadlyme, CT 06439
860 526-9836

Douglas Garofalo
Garofalo Architects
3752 North Ashland Avenue
Chicago, IL 60613
773 975-2069
dougg@uic.edu

Patrick Pinnell Architect
225 Fairfield Avenue
Hartford, CT
860 956-9244

James Ezzes
31 Prospect Road
Westport, CT 06880
203 227-4861

Paul Harris
Cole Harris Associates
175 Post Road West
Westport, CT 06880
203 226-1830

Stuart Disston
Austin Patterson Disston Architects
376 Pequot Avenue
Southport, CT 06490
203 255-4031

Christopher Carpiniello Architect
30 Blue Ridge Lane
Wilton, CT 06897
203 762-5953

Robert Harper Architect
38 Oak Drive
Centerbrook, CT 06409
860 767-0629
rpharper@connix.com

Robert Orr & Associates, LLC
441 Chapel Street
New Haven, CT 06511
203 777-3387

A.D. Ialeggio Associates
166 Kings Highway North
Westport, CT 06880
203 227-3846

Susan Albright Design Inc.
213 Greens Farms Road
Westport, CT 06880
(203) 259-1478

James Estes and Company Architects
79 Thames Street
Newport, RI 02840
401 846-3336

Jeffrey Rowe
Stratfield Builders
1316 Stratfield Avenue
Fairfield, CT 06432
203 372-0202

Michael Farewell
Ford Farewell Mills and Gatsch
864 Mapleton Road
Princeton, New Jersey 08540
609 452-1777

David Preusch Architect
15 Imperial Avenue
Westport, CT 06880
203 221-8371

Duo Dickinson Architect
94 Bradley Road
Madison, CT 06443
203 245-0405
duo.dickinson@snet.net

Craig Saunders
DuBose Associates, Inc. Architects
49 Woodland Street
Hartford, CT 06105
860 249-9387

Helen Theurkauf & Company
2027 Main Street
Glastonbury, CT 06033
860 633-2420